D0792367

Children of the World

Indonesia

For their help in the preparation of *Children of the World: Indonesia,* the editors gratefully thank Harry (Sony) Miarsono and Siu Tjen, Milwaukee; the Embassy of Indonesia (US), Washington DC; the International Institute of Wisconsin, Milwaukee; the United States Department of State, Bureau of Public Affairs, Office of Public Communication, Washington, DC, for unencumbered use of material in the public domain; the Canadian Department of External Affairs, Ottawa, Ont.; the Canadian Department of Employment and Immigration, Ottawa, Ont.; the US Immigration and Naturalization Service, Washington, DC; Sita Adishakti, Milwaukee.

Library of Congress Cataloging-in-Publication Data

Tozuka, Takako.
  Indonesia.

  (Children of the world)
  Bibliography: p.
  Includes index.
  Summary: Presents the life of an eleven-year-old boy and his family living in Krawang, Indonesia, describing his home and school, daily activities, and the festivals, religious ceremonies, and national holidays of his country.
    1. Indonesia—Juvenile literature.   2. Children—
Indonesia—Juvenile literature.   [1. Indonesia—Social
life and customs.   2. Family life—Indonesia]
I. Knowlton, Marylee, 1946-   II. Sachner, Mark,
1948-   III. Title.   IV. Series.
DS615.T68   1987   959.8'038   86-42807
ISBN 1-55532-190-9
ISBN 1-55532-165-8 (lib. bdg.)

North American edition first published in 1987 by

Gareth Stevens, Inc.
7317 West Green Tree Road   Milwaukee, Wisconsin 53223, USA

This work was originally published in shortened form consisting of section I only.
Photographs and original text copyright © 1986 by Takako Tozuka.
First and originally published by Kaisei-sha Publishing Co., Ltd., Tokyo.
World English rights arranged with Kaisei-sha Publishing Co., Ltd. through Japan Foreign-Rights Centre.

Typeset by Ries Graphics ltd., Milwaukee.
Design: Laurie Shock and Leanne Dillingham.
Map design: Gary Moseley.

2   3   4   5   6   7   8   9   92   91   90   89   88

Children of the World

Indonesia

Photography by
Takako Tozuka

Edited by
MaryLee Knowlton &
Mark J. Sachner

Gareth Stevens Publishing
Milwaukee

. . . a note about *Children of the World*:

The children of the world live in fishing towns and urban centers, on islands and in mountain valleys, on sheep ranches and fruit farms. This series follows one child in each country through the pattern of his or her life. Candid photographs show the children with their families, at school, at play, and in their communities. The text describes the dreams of the children and, often through their own words, tells how they see themselves and their lives.

Each book also explores events that are unique to the country in which the child lives, including festivals, religious ceremonies, and national holidays. The *Children of the World* series does more than tell about foreign countries. It introduces the children of each country and shows readers what it is like to be a child in that country.

. . . and about *Indonesia*:

Eleven-year-old Doni and his family have recently moved from Jakarta to a larger house near the tracks in Krawang. Here Doni and his four brothers and sisters play and go to school. His father works for the railroad, just as Doni hopes to do someday. Doni's life is a busy one. In fact, his day begins before sunrise, when the many street vendors make their first appearance with their wares.

To enhance this book's value in libraries and classrooms, comprehensive reference sections include up-to-date data about Indonesia's geography, demographics, language, currency, education, culture, industry, and natural resources. *Indonesia* also features a bibliography, research topics, activity projects, and discussions of such subjects as Jakarta, the country's history, political system, ethnic and religious composition, and language.

The living conditions and experiences of children in Indonesia vary tremendously according to economic, environmental, and ethnic circumstances. The reference sections help bring to life for young readers the diversity and richness of the culture and heritage of Indonesia. Of particular interest are discussions of the relations among Indonesia's hundreds of minority cultures and national groups, all of whom have made their presence felt in the languages — also in the hundreds — and traditions of Indonesia.

CONTENTS

The backyard of Doni's house. Children from the neighborhood often come over to play.

LIVING IN INDONESIA:
Doni, a Life with Trains

Meet Doni, an 11-year-old boy from Indonesia. Indonesia is a country of 13,500 islands scattered north and south of the equator. Doni lives with his family on Jawa, or Java, the country's central island. They recently moved to the village of Krawang from Jakarta, Indonesia's capital. Doni's family consists of eight people — five children, their parents, and their grandmother.

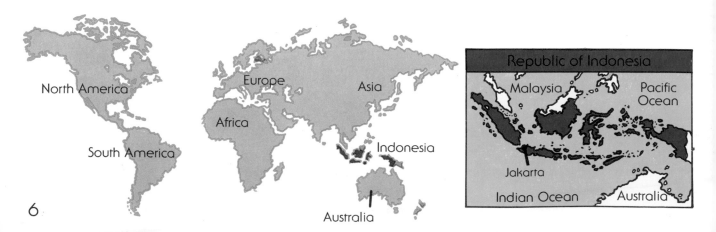

6

Doni and his older brother, Agus, and younger brother Ali. The street in front of their house is a busy one, with lots of traffic. The street also has lots of potholes, and whenever it rains, they become muddy puddles.

Some train tracks that run through Krawang. The tracks are a busy place for people and animals alike.

The tracks near Krawang Station. A train comes from Jakarta every two hours. There have been trains in Indonesia for over 100 years. Still, only the islands of Java, Sumatra, and Madura have rail service.

In Krawang, Doni's family now has a larger house and a yard big enough for soccer practice. The house is located between the railroad tracks and the rice fields. Doni's mother and grandmother love the new house because it has a well in the kitchen. In Jakarta, they had to carry water from a common well. The children love the two extra rooms and the large yard with five banana trees. The yard also has a *nangka,* or jack fruit tree. It produces a fruit much like an apple.

Most locomotive engines in Indonesia are made in West Germany or Japan.

Doni loves to watch trains at the station in Krawang.

All day and night Doni can hear the trains run by their house. Doni has been looking at trains every day since he was a tiny boy. He wants to get a job on the railway just like his father, who works for the Indonesian National Railway. Doni's father is a communications engineer. His working hours change, and he has to travel four hours a day between Jakarta, where he works, and Krawang. Many people in Indonesia are unemployed.

Family Life

Today Doni's father is home for dinner. It isn't often that the whole family can eat together. They have *nasi goreng*, or fried rice with onions, chicken, hot red peppers, ajinomoto, and soy sauce. It takes only five minutes to cook. Often Doni makes it for himself.

Nasi goreng, one of Indonesia's most popular dishes.

Many Indonesians, like Doni and his father, use knives and forks when they eat. But others, like his mother, have kept the custom of eating with their hands.

13

Doni's father fixes the TV antenna. The children look for ways to help.

Kneeling on the kitchen floor, Doni's mother fixes dinner on their stove.

Today is Doni's father's day off. But he discovers that his children have big plans for him. Today he must put up the TV antenna. They have lived in the new house for four months now, and he hasn't had time to fix it. Today he has time, and the children help.

Indonesian TV has only one channel and not many programs for children. But after four months, Doni is happy that he can watch his favorite shows.

Doni with his most treasured possessions. This phone is linked to the phones of other railway employees. ▶

15

The children launch their kites without any strings.

The Children at Play

From the field in back of the house come the happy cries of children flying kites. Children in Indonesia love flying kites all year round. The kites don't have strings to hang onto, but they soar high in the sky anyway. Sometimes a kite will fall and get caught in a tree. When this happens, the children become excited and crowd around the tree. Someone will always run up from behind to remove the kite from the tree with a long stick.

More fun in the field behind Doni's house — soccer.

Doni's favorite game is soccer. He gets so excited that he keeps running after the ball even after his sandals have slipped off.

Doni, Agus, and Ali enjoy their comic books. Their youngest brother, Budi, and their sister, Dewi, keep them company.

Doni loves to read. He enjoys many kinds of books, but he especially loves to read comics. Comic book shops are found all over town, even in the schools. The books cost 150 *rupiah*, and Doni and his brother Agus take turns buying copies. They let their younger brother Ali read them, too. They read the same comics again and again, and they save even the old worn-out copies.

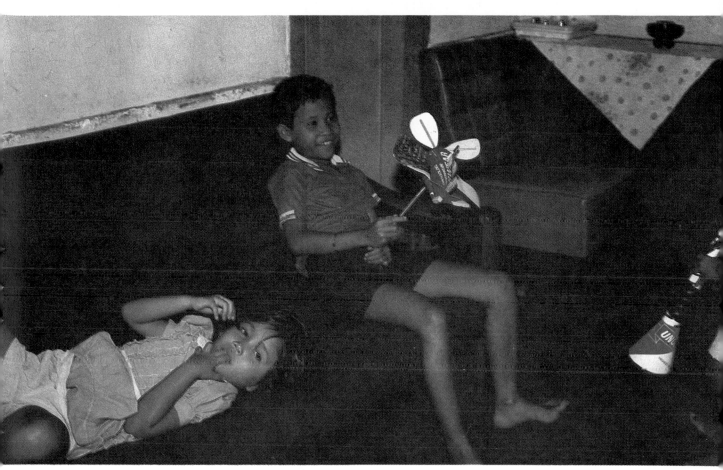

Doni with his "best friend," Dewi. In the rainy season, the children play indoors most of the time.

Doni's mother sometimes tells him that he spends too much time with his comics. So Doni has a secret place for reading, up in the nangka tree in the backyard. He can sit up there for hours, reading and eating the tree's sweet fruit. Today as he was heading for the tree, his young sister, Dewi, followed him. So he came back in the house so she wouldn't discover his hideout.

For Doni, the entire area around the train station is a big playground.

Doni has another secret place, a cabin where the railroad switches are changed. Nobody but the signal point men are supposed to go into this cabin. But Doni is friends with one of the men. When he's on duty, the man lets Doni in. This is Doni's favorite place to be. From the big window upstairs, Doni has a great view. He can see all the trains coming in and going out of the station.

On the coupling car in the railroad yard, the
boys pretend to be railroad engineers.

Doni and his brothers and friends also climb up on the
coupling car parked near the cabin. They pretend that the
coupling car is a big locomotive engine and that they are
railroad engineers. The whole area around the station turns
into a playground. *Everything* about trains is exciting to Doni.

Doni and his brothers drop into the toy shop on the way home.

Doni can't play all the time. He has homework to do. But before he settles down, he has a couple of stops to make. First is the toy store. It is filled with toys and games. Some toys, such as plastic models, cars, and robots, are from Japan and other foreign countries. Doni wishes there were more toy trains.

Every day Doni drops into the toy shop for just a few minutes. Then he heads for his next stop.

Next door to the toy shop is the comic book shop. Sometimes Doni also stops at the grocery shop or at a shop where he can buy notebooks and other school supplies. But usually the comic book shop is his last stop before homework. He takes his time looking through the comics till he finds one that he doesn't have yet. The shopowner knows all the children because they come in at least once a day. He lets them browse as long as they like.

Buying notebooks at the stationery shop.

Just about everything is sold at the grocery shop — even belts!

A baker.

A meat vendor.

A bottled water vendor.

The Wonderful World of Peddlers

At four o'clock in the morning, the mist is still hanging low. Doni wakes up to the sound of a loudspeaker from the local mosque, an Islamic temple. It calls people to morning prayers. He also hears a bell-like sound passing in front of the house. It is the rice cereal vendor, who walks around tapping the edge of a bowl with a spoon. This is how he tells people he has rice cereal to sell.

Doni also hears the cry "Roti! Roti!" *Roti* is bread, and the cry comes from the baker. He is pulling a cart loaded with breads and with cakes filled with chocolate and custard.

A toffee vendor.

A mattress vendor.

In Indonesia peddlers are everywhere. They are in the streets, the markets, even the open fields. Many sell things to eat, such as candy or fried bananas, called *pisang goreng*. Some sell herb medicines and bottled water. Some carry all kinds of hardware goods, such as brooms, scrubbing pads, strainers, baskets, and pots and pans that have been broken and fixed. Some even sell mattresses, which usually come in pairs.

These vendors come from the countryside. They help make the town lively and fun. In a developing country like Indonesia, many people work at jobs that the government calls "informal." Peddling goods is one of these jobs.

A vendor peddling *pisang goreng,* or fried bananas.

25

A tofu noodle vendor.

A *jamu*, or herb medicine, vendor.

Doni's favorite — mie bakso.

As the day heats up, the children's favorite vendors come through the streets. First is the ice cream man, making a pon-pon sound. Next comes a juice vendor carrying different flavors of juice. Their calls fill the street. The children hear them, and they come dashing out of their houses and run straight to the vendors. Doni can tell the difference between the vendors by the sounds they make in the street.

Doni's favorite food is *mie bakso,* a noodle soup with meatballs. Doni does not get an allowance. So when he hears the mie bakso vendor striking his bamboo cylinder, he begs his mother for change for food. Doni's family is quite informal about meals. Often the children prepare their own food or buy it from vendors.

Today Doni eats his breakfast at home. Sometimes he buys his breakfast from a vendor on the way. Many of his meals come from vendors.

Some students walk to school on the tracks.

At School

Doni's school is the Budimekar No. 2 Primary School. It is near the train tracks, only a three-minute walk from his house. Doni is in the 5th grade, and he walks to school with his good friend Tono, who is in the 4th grade.

In Indonesia the public schools do not have enough classrooms, and the same buildings have to be used by two different schools. One meets in the morning hours and the other in the afternoon. Doni's school shares its buildings with Budimekar No. 3 School. The two schools change morning and afternoon sessions every week. This week Doni's school is on the morning schedule.

Doni leaves for school. He says good-bye to his family by kissing the hands of his grandmother and parents in the proper order. First he kisses his grandmother's hand, then his father's, and then his mother's.

School is only a three-minute walk from home.

Doni's fifth grade teacher, Miss Nurayati, teaches all the subjects
except religion and physical education.

Children arrive at school before seven. In front of the school
gate are noodle vendors and stalls where tofu and bananas
are deep-fried to the spitting sound of hot oil. Some children
are buying and eating this food. Doni has eaten at home, so
he walks quickly among the vendors. But he is already thinking
of eating mie bakso during the class break.

This morning the first class is math. Adding fractions is currently
Doni's biggest headache. His favorite subject is Bahasa
Indonesia, the national language. The school also gives classes
in the Sundanese language, since many Sundanese people
live in Krawang. Doni and his family are Sundanese, the
second largest people in a country of over 400 peoples. They
speak the Sundanese language at home.

Doni's classroom. There are seven class periods a day. Each one lasts 40 minutes.

The school gate is crowded with vendors.

Doni and his classmates also study the Arabic language. They must know Arabic to read the Islamic teachings for their religion class. According to the nation's Five Principles, religion must be taught in school. Called *Pancasila,* these principles were formed by the country's first president, Sukarno. He believed that religious belief encouraged strong values and national pride following the nation's independence in 1945.

A group picture of Doni and some of his classmates. Krawang is mainly Muslim, so Arabic and Islam are taught in public school.

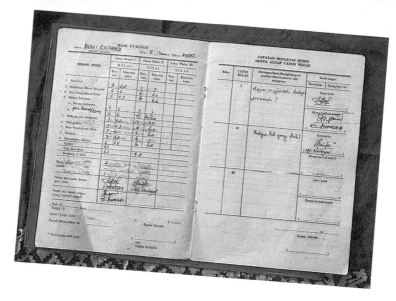

Each student has his or her own report book. In it, his or her school record is kept over six years. The book also contains a photo of the student and the school's seal. Some report books contain the student's thumbprint.

In home economics class, the students are free to move around and help one another.

Volleyball practice.

During class break, Doni and Ali enjoy their favorite, mie bakso.

The last class before the break is home economics. The students lend each other scissors and needles. They teach each other how to use them and make handkerchiefs.

The moment class is over, Doni dashes out of the classroom to the noodle stall at the school gate. He and his younger brother Ali meet at the vendor. They eat their mie bakso together. Other children crowd around ice cream and cracker stalls.

The school grounds are pitted with puddles, so the children play in the hall.

An after-school Boy Scout training meeting.

Doni and his fellow Boy Scouts study their Scout rule books.

The last class of the day is physical education. The students do exercises to the music of a tape recorder. Then they play volleyball. Besides their seven classes a day, the boys have Boy Scout meetings twice a week after school. All boys in Indonesia must be Boy Scouts starting in fourth grade.

The school grounds become a marketplace just for kids.

A passion for ice cream!

Honeyed millet is a favorite of these girls.

The school year starts one week after the end of the Islamic month of fasting known as Ramadan. Because it is based on the Muslim calendar, Ramadan ends at a different time each year. So the school schedule must be adjusted each year.

Some of the students at the Budimekar No. 2 Primary School.

Another shop sells patches, stickers, comics, and stereoscopic viewers.

A fried-potato vendor.

Doni investigates a candy shop on the school grounds.

As a marketplace, the pasar is smaller than the large shopping centers in the cities and larger than the rural roadside stalls. Here the food is fresh, and you can bargain for lower prices.

Krawang — a Busy Town

In Indonesia even the smallest villages have a *pasar,* or marketplace, at their center. The pasar in Krawang is just down the street from Doni's house. The vendors' call to their customers — "Yo! Yo!" — echoes throughout the pasar. Doni loves to go with his mother to hear her bargain with the vendors. Vendors and customers argue over the prices of everything until both are satisfied.

In this tropical country there is a lot of fruit. Durian, the king of fruit, is as large as a child's head. It looks awful and smells worse. But it tastes delicious. The queen of fruit is the mangosteen, which looks like a persimmon and has a soft and sweet white pulp. Bananas come in many varieties, from large green to small orange.

Goldfish.

Herbs.

Pisang goreng — fried bananas.

Colorful cakes.

Salted mangoes and other foods.

Prepared and dried foods.

A common well in Krawang.

Doni helps his mother give Budi and Dewi a bath.

Doni helps his mother shop for rice, one of Indonesia's staple foods.

Doni often walks his father to the train station at 6 a.m.

Doni and his friend Tono chat with a police officer.

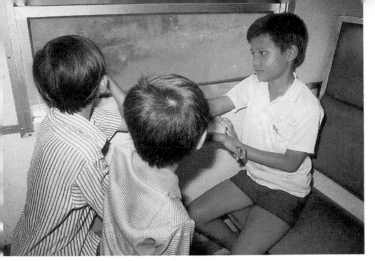

Riding the rails to Cikampek.

Cikampek Station: A place for people and animals alike!

Krawang Station: Rickshaws wait for passengers.

Riding the Rails

The families of National Railways workers get a free pass for train rides. Doni and his brothers and friends often ride the trains to the neighboring town of Cikampek. The peddlers hop on along the way, carrying their wares to market. There are three different classes of train cars. In the third class cars, the human passengers are sometimes joined by goats and chickens.

The boys enjoy their day in Cikampek. The town is much like Krawang. But the trainyard has examples of steam engines, called "kereta api," which means "fire wheels." They are rare now in Indonesia, where most of the trains are either diesel or electric.

41

The streets in Krawang at dusk.

Coming Home

Most Indonesians are Muslim, and a call for prayer is given from the town mosques five times a day. People stop what they are doing to pray while facing in the direction of Mecca, the holy city of Islam. On Fridays, Islamic people visit their mosques. Doni wears a *kain*, which is a wrap skirt, and a *topi*, which is a black hat, for these religious services. Women are not allowed in the mosques, so his mother prays at home.

Enjoying the evening with friends in the fields behind the house.

Praying at the mosque, Doni wears a kain and a topi for his prayers as he faces Mecca to the west.

The children of Indonesia are taught the Koran from a very young age. Doni's mother teaches him one page a week. The Koran teaches children to help each other and their parents. Doni shows he has learned its teachings by looking after his younger brothers and sister and cleaning the concrete floor of their home every day.

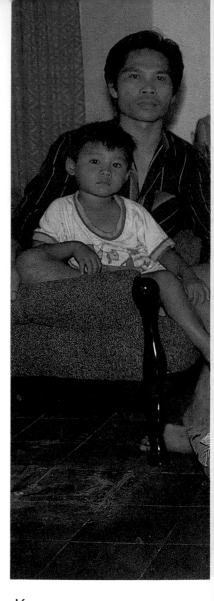

Doni's father helps him with math.

The seven o'clock train from Jakarta has arrived in Krawang loaded with passengers. Among them is Doni's father. As soon as he gets home, he takes a shower, or *mandi,* with water from the water tank. In this humid country, people often take three or four showers a day.

Refreshed and relaxed, Doni's father checks his son's homework. Patiently he explains where Doni has gone wrong with his fractions. To work for the railway like his father, Doni will have to go to an engineering high school. So he struggles hard with his math, though it is not his favorite subject.

44

A portrait of Doni's family, plus one.

Tonight the whole family gathers in the living room for a family portrait. A neighbor drops in to visit, and she has her picture taken, too. The younger children fall asleep to the sound of friendly voices talking softly. The whistle of the last train of the day is heard passing by.

The children of Indonesia at work and at play.

46

FOR YOUR INFORMATION: Indonesia

Official Name: Republic of Indonesia

Capital: Jakarta

History

Indonesia: *"Bhinneka Tunggal Ika"* — "Unity in Diversity"

Indonesia: long a meeting ground for many nations and peoples of Asia, the East Indies, and Europe. Modern Indonesia encompasses hundreds of racial and national groups, dozens of languages and dialects, and an archipelago, or chain, of over 13,000 islands. These islands stretch 3200 miles (5120 km) from east to west, and 1000 miles (1600 km) from north to south, between the Indian and Pacific Oceans. And with its history of empires, colonial and mercantile exploitation, and revolution and independence, Indonesia is still a country of countries, a nation of national groups.

Prehistoric Indonesia

In 1890, a Dutch physician discovered a jawbone in Central Java. This jawbone — labeled "Java Man" — belonged to a member of the species *Homo erectus. Homo erectus*, a direct ancestor of modern *Homo sapiens*, or man, is thought to have lived between 250,000 and 1.7 million years ago. According to fossilized evidence, modern *Homo sapiens* dates back 40,000 or more years in Indonesia. Evidence of human burials and cremations from 20,000 years ago, cave paintings, pottery, and huge monuments are all signs of prehistoric cultures in Indonesia over tens of thousands of years. The remains of these cultures have given us clues about how we humans developed into what we are today.

Indonesia's Hindu, Buddhist, and Muslim Empires

Indonesia's recorded history did not begin until the 7th century AD. Prior to this time, Indonesia was inhabited by aboriginal groups, mostly in southern Sumatra, and groups who migrated from Asia. Art showing East Indian touches and pictures of Chinese dress mean that there was much trade throughout Indonesia by 200-100 BC. There is also evidence of Hindu and Buddhist influence in Indonesia from 200 AD on, and the first references to Indonesian kingdoms appear in Chinese and Indian writings dating from the 5th century AD. For centuries, Indian culture and religion dominated parts of the East Indies, and some of Indonesia's early kingdoms were Hindu, while others were Buddhist.

"Indianized" Indonesia produced two of the region's most powerful empires. One was the Buddhist kingdom of Sriwijaya in Sumatra from the 12th to the 14th centuries. In the 14th century, the Hindu kingdom of Majapahit had its capital in eastern Java. Javanese civilization reached its height in the 14th century, and both Buddhist and Hindu states left temples that are among the world's most impressive examples of ancient art.

Arab, Indian, and Malay traders brought Islam to the region in the 12th century. By the 15th century there were small Muslim states all along the Indonesian coasts. With the coming of Islam, Java's Hindu culture retreated to Bali, where Hinduism thrives to this day.

Prambanan, the largest Hindu temple in Indonesia. Its ancient remains are a major tourist stop in Yogyakarta, Java.

Under European Colonialism

Fragmented into many small states, the once-powerful kingdoms were unable to resist Western colonialism. The Portuguese began to trade in the Indonesian "Spice Islands," and in 1511 they conquered the Muslim kingdom of Malacca, in Malaya. The Dutch began to take over Indonesia by the early 1600s, however. The Dutch East India Companies had a trade empire centered in Batavia, now Jakarta, on Java. By 1700, the Dutch were in control of almost all of Indonesia. East Timor stayed Portuguese until it became part of Indonesia in 1976; Indonesia came briefly under British rule from 1811 to 1816; and the Japanese occupied Indonesia briefly for three years during World War II. Otherwise, Indonesia would be the Netherlands East Indies for 300 years, until World War II.

Resistance and Independence

During their brief takeover in 1811, the British did away with the harsh Dutch system of forced labor. When the Dutch regained control in 1816, Indonesian resistance to colonial rule had begun. Even as Holland developed the East Indies into one of the world's richest colonial possessions, Dutch rule was an uneasy one. The Indonesian independence movement began in the early 20th century and grew quickly between World War I and II. Before World War II, the Dutch imprisoned many of the resistance leaders, including the future first president of Indonesia, Sukarno. In 1945, three days after the Japanese surrender, a small group led by Sukarno declared Indonesia's independence and formed the Republic of Indonesia.

On December 27, 1949, after four years of bitter war, rule was finally transferred to the Indonesians. The next year, Indonesia became the 60th member of the United Nations. In 1963, the Dutch gave up their last East Indies territory, Dutch New Guinea, or Irian Jaya. In 1975, events in Portugal forced that country's withdrawal from East Timor, a Portuguese colony for four centuries. A power struggle among several Timorese factions led Indonesia to send in troops of its own, and in 1976 East Timor became Indonesia's 27th province.

Sukarno

Indonesia has had a stormy independence. From 1949-1959, Indonesia went through several island rebellions and an unsuccessful attempt at parliamentary government. In 1959, President Sukarno decreed that the executive branch would have supreme power in the government, as it had under the 1945 constitution. Sukarno gave many Indonesians a feeling of national pride, and he is a hero to the Indonesian people today. But his domestic and foreign policies made him a controversial leader. During the 1960s, Sukarno aligned Indonesia with Asian communist states, encouraged the political role of the Indonesian Communist Party, the PKI, and challenged Malaysia militarily following that country's independence in 1963.

In 1965, the army resisted efforts to arm Sukarno's supporters among the PKI. On September 30, 1965, the PKI attempted to seize power. By the next day, October 1, the army had defeated the attempt. PKI supporters assassinated several army generals, and by February 1966 hundreds of thousands of Indonesians were killed in a cycle of violence and retaliation. The shock of the violence created emotions among Indonesia's many religious and national groups that are still alive today. Sukarno attempted to restore things to how they were before October, but with little success. Unable to control the political situation, Sukarno stepped down and chose Suharto to be acting president on March 11, 1966. Out of the national scene, Sukarno died in 1970.

Suharto

Suharto became Indonesia's *elected* president, and he has been elected to 5-year terms through the present. Suharto had led the defeat of the PKI uprising. His government is dominated by the military but receives advice from economic experts. His primary goal has been Indonesia's economic development. Many Indonesians today hope that the country's return to parliamentary democracy will stabilize the government, further reduce the role of the military, and improve the lives of Indonesians of every religion, national group, and region.

Population and Ethnic Groups

Indonesia's total 1985 population was around 170 million people. This makes Indonesia the fifth most populous nation in the world, behind China, India, the Soviet Union, and the US. With a population of over 80 million, the island of Java alone is one of the most densely populated areas in the world. The government has tried to move people away from overcrowded Java and Bali to the less crowded outer islands. Called the transmigration program, it has been quite controversial and has had limited success. Indonesia has hundreds of national groups, many of them ethnic Malays.

The more numerous peoples include the Javanese, Sundanese, Madurese, coastal Malays, Batak, Buginese, Minangkabau, Irian Jayans, and Balinese. The Chinese are the largest non-Malay minority. Relations between the ethnic Chinese and Indonesia's majority Malay peoples have at times been strained. As in Malaysia, the Chinese live mainly in the cities and hold more economic than political power. In the early 1980s, fighting broke out between ethnic Chinese and other national groups on Java.

Each group has its own culture, language, and traditions. These traditions are known among ethnic Malays as the *adat*, or "custom," of a community. Some Indonesians identify so strongly with the adat of their group that these customs become themselves the basis for their ethnic identity. For example, to an ethnic Malay, merely converting to Islam may be regarded as *masuk Melayu*, or having "entered the Malay fold." Among Javanese, a child who does not yet understand the values and feelings of its elders may be called *durung Jawa* — not yet Javanese. And a Balinese who stops worshipping as a Hindu and converts to Christianity or Islam may be said to be no longer Balinese.

Religion

Four religions are officially recognized and guaranteed religious freedom: Islam, Christianity, Hinduism, and Buddhism. Indonesia is about 90% Muslim, 5% Christian, and 3% Hindu. Christianity is strong in some of the northern areas, while the island of Bali has stayed mainly Hindu. Buddhism and Confucianism are also practiced, mainly among the ethnic Chinese minority. Also, many of the native peoples of Borneo, or Kalimantan, and of Irian Jaya have traditional religious or spiritual beliefs. Many combine these beliefs with Indonesia's official religions.

Even Muslims, Christians, Hindus, and Buddhists mix their primary religious beliefs with other religions and local traditions. These traditions and practices, called *adat*, or "custom," are often of greater value to a local group than the religion itself. For example, a Javanese who considers himself or herself a Muslim may also believe in Hindu gods and in the folk heroes and gods portrayed in a *wayang* shadow play. Or a Balinese who is Hindu may worship in a Hindu temple dedicated to both Hindu gods and Balinese nature spirits. Religion in Indonesia connects people with their common ancestors, folklore, and present situations.

Government

Indonesia is a republic based on a constitution developed in 1945. The constitution provides for a limited separation of powers between the three branches of the government: executive, legislative, and judicial. The president is elected for a 5-year term by the legislature. He has a cabinet of 37 ministers who represent different segments of the population. The legislature operates differently from Western legislatures. It meets only once in 5 years to set long-term goals and to elect the president and vice president. The court system differs from Western systems as well. In Indonesia, judges are part of the executive branch because they are government employees. In the West, they are part of the judicial branch.

In the past, the government of Indonesia has been unstable because of deep divisions between various ethnic and religious groups. The current government has taken steps to limit the power of these groups. Indonesia's motto is "*Bhinneka Tunggal Ika,*" which means "Unity in Diversity." The military, which has 370,000 members, is powerful in Indonesia. As in many newly developing countries, the military supports the government. Without its support the government will fall. In recent years economic specialists educated in the West have made policies and run programs.

The major political group in Indonesia is GOLKAR, a coalition of government employees, young people, labor, farmers, and women. As the majority group, GOLKAR controls the legislature.

Indonesia is divided into 27 provinces and subdivided into 281 regencies. The governors and regents of these areas are appointed by the president. Many provinces are isolated geographically, culturally, and politically from the government in Jakarta. East Timor, for example, has been a province since 1976, when Indonesia took it over from Portugal. Since then, it has suffered from underdevelopment, famine, and, some argue, neglect by the Indonesian government.

In the years after its independence, Indonesia was anti-Western and especially anti-US. The current government has friendlier relations with the West. It still maintains an independent stance, though, and is a nonaligned nation. It has provided temporary sanctuary for many Indochinese refugees.

Language

Since Indonesia's independence, Bahasa Indonesia has been the official national language. The roots of Bahasa Indonesia are Malay. But it is also a modern language, with many new words. Today, Bahasa Indonesia is the official written language and the language of business, education, and government. So far, however, only about 40% of the population uses Bahasa Indonesia. Local groups still use their native languages and dialects, and many older people speak Dutch. Of the local languages, Javanese is the most widely spoken. English is by far the most widely spoken foreign language and is taught from 7th grade through university.

In Malaysia, the official language is called Bahasa Malaysia. It is virtually identical to Bahasa Indonesia.

Currency

The chief monetary unit in Indonesia is the *rupiah*. It comes in denominations of 100, 500, 1000, 2000, 5000, and 10,000 rupiah bills, and 1, 5, 10, 25, 50, and 100 rupiah coins.

Arts and Crafts

In Indonesia, each linguistic and ethnic group has its own unique performing arts. These arts reflect the values and traditions of the culture.

Drama in Indonesia is called *wayang*. It combines music, dance, and story within two traditions, the village and court theater. Within both traditions there are puppet theater, shadow plays, and mask dances. All are based on ancient Indian and Javanese tales.

A *wayang orang* show in Java. *Orang* means "human." *Wayang kulit* uses puppets.

Tribal dances mark life rituals such as births, marriages, deaths, and harvests. They also mark tribal functions like changing leaders, moving the village, preparing for battle, and celebrating victory. The *barong* of Bali is a dance drama in which the dancers fall into a trance as they act out an ancient story. They are released from the trance after the villagers offer a sacrifice to the spirits. On Java the *Kuda Kepang*, or hobbyhorse dance, is performed in the markets. This too results in a trance for the dancers. They ride into the marketplace on bamboo or leather hobbyhorses. Some begin to act like horses, racing around and eating straw, until they are released from the trance.

Of the court dances, the most famous is the *Bedoya Ketawang*. This is a sacred and secret dance performed once a year in the Surakarta palace by nine female palace guards. It is believed to come from ancient fertility rituals.

The music of the *gamelan*, the orchestra, of Bali and Java accompanies all types of dance, dance dramas, and puppet shows. Some say it is the sound of moonlight. In the quiet of the night, its bronze gongs and drums can be heard for miles, echoing solemnly. A Javanese or Balinese audience knows from the music which battle will be fought on stage or which character is about to appear.

The gamelan musicians play bronze percussion instruments, gongs, and drums. They also play *kendhang*, or wooden drums, the *suling*, which is a bamboo flute, and the *rebab*, a two stringed lute or fiddle. The gamelan of Bali is lively and exciting. The Javanese gamelan is majestic and slow.

The performing arts in Indonesia are elaborate and expensive to perform. Today they are supported largely by tourists. Performers are dedicated to their arts but usually have other jobs unless they perform in tourist areas.

Industry, Agriculture, and Natural Resources

A Growing Economy

Indonesia is rich in natural resources, including oil, natural gas, and iron. Many of its resources are underdeveloped, and agriculture is still the major source of employment and production, putting to work about 60% of the labor force.

Indonesia is self-sufficient in rice and is the world's third largest producer of rice. Indonesia is also the second largest in world rubber production and fifth largest in soybean and timber production. The government sees greater rubber and palm oil crops as a source of increased exports and higher employment. Sugar and coffee are also major agricultural exports. More than 60% of the nation's income is from government-owned oil production. But the world's oil market is unstable at times, and oil cannot be counted on as a source of future revenue. Indonesia's major customers are Japan, the US, and Singapore, and its major suppliers are Japan, the US, and Thailand.

Textiles — Industry and Art Form

Textiles, one of Indonesia's principal exports, are also a significant Indonesian art form. Indonesia makes more kinds of textiles than any other country in the world. Some say that all 350-400 linguistic and ethnic groups have their own textile traditions. Some of these traditions are more than 2000 years old. Many have been influenced by Indonesia's long history of foreign trade and migration, especially from India and Europe. The textiles represent more than just colored cloth. The different designs and materials symbolize power and status. Throughout history, they have been used as gifts to the gods and to friends, even to enemies. The making and giving of the cloths have been surrounded by taboos, beliefs, and magic.

Spinning, dyeing, and weaving symbolized creation. These tasks were, and still are, done by women. Men were allowed to dye only a few threads. The dyeing was done in great secrecy. The dyes were complex and carefully guarded.

Many of the designs have spiritual meaning. Most famous is the theme on the ship cloths. A ship, or sometimes a bird, represents the passage of time. The cloth was used at life rituals such as birth, circumcision, marriage, and death. Certain cloths, colors, and themes were used only for royalty.

From Borneo comes the *fuja*, or barkcloth. Sumatra weaves *sonket* silks, gleaming fabrics shot through with gold and silver threads. *Ikats*, complex tie-dyed cloths, come from the eastern islands. And, of course, there are the beautiful *batiks* from Java.

Batik — an Indonesian Original

The art of batik began in Indonesia. It is done now in many other countries, even the US and Canada. But the batik of Indonesia is the most beautiful. It begins with a white cloth, either cotton or silk. The artist sketches the design directly onto the cloth. Then she covers the areas not to be dyed with wax. She soaks the cloth in the dye and lets it dry. Sometimes the cloth is dyed and dried many times till it takes on the hue the artist wants. Next it is boiled or scraped to remove the wax in preparation for the next color. Then parts not to be dyed in the second color are waxed, and the cloth is dyed and dried again. This process is repeated for each color.

The Indonesian batik industry catalogues over 1000 traditional designs. At one time everyone in Indonesia wore batik. Today many young Indonesians prefer Western-style clothes and the wrinkle-free ease of polyester. Still, a market exists in the West, where fashion leaders use batik in clothing and furniture fabrics. The industry has switched to faster, synthetic dyes with a wider variety of colors.

Land

Indonesia is an archipelago, or chain, of islands stretching from the Malay Peninsula of Southeast Asia east toward Australia. With over 13,500 islands, it is the world's largest archipelago. Many of these islands are quite small, but over 3,000 are large enough to be inhabited. Indonesia shares Borneo with East Malaysia, and it shares New Guinea with Papua New Guinea. In addition to its land borders with Malaysia and Papua New Guinea, Indonesia shares sea borders with Singapore, Vietnam, the Philippines, and Australia.

The entire Indonesian archipelago stretches over 3200 miles (5120 km). This means that Indonesia would stretch across North America all the way from Oregon in the Pacific Northwest to Bermuda in the Atlantic. Of all this area, about two-thirds is made up of ocean connecting the islands. The total land area of Indonesia is 735,000 sq miles (1.88 million sq km). This makes it the world's seventh largest nation in land size, behind the USSR, Canada, China, the US, Brazil, and Australia.

Except for Borneo, which is geologically quite stable, just about all of Indonesia's islands are volcanic. Hundreds of volcanoes dot Indonesia's landscape. Over 70 of them are active, and just about each year there is a major eruption. In 1982, an eruption in West Java killed many people. The eruption of Krakatau in 1884 is one of the world's best known. But the largest eruption in recorded history took place in 1815 on the island of Sumbawa. Mt. Tambora's eruption killed 90,000 people. It ejected so much volcanic matter that it blocked the sun for many months.

Climate

Indonesia is a tropical or equatorial country, and most of it is surrounded by water. Its climate is therefore equatorial. This means that distance and seasonal change do not affect Indonesia's weather as much as do landscape, altitude, and rainfall. At sea level, temperatures are generally in the 80s Fahrenheit (20-30 range Centigrade) year-round, and there is a great deal of humidity. But in the mountains, the temperature falls about two degrees Fahrenheit (one degree Centigrade) for every 656 ft (200 m) of altitude. This makes the climate quite pleasant in higher towns like Bandung in Java. At 3000 ft (900 m), Bandung has temperatures that fall comfortably into the middle to high 70s F (around 25°C).

In many parts of the Indonesian archipelago, several inches of rain fall per month. During the northeast monsoon season, from November to March, wet winds from the South China Sea drench parts of Indonesia. West Java gets as much as 200 inches (400 cm) annually. The southeast monsoon brings hot, dry wind up from Australia. This gives many islands a dry season from April to October, and some islands, such as Timor and Sumba, have long dry spells that can lead to two-year droughts. During the southeast monsoon, southeastern Java and southern Bali are also quite dry.

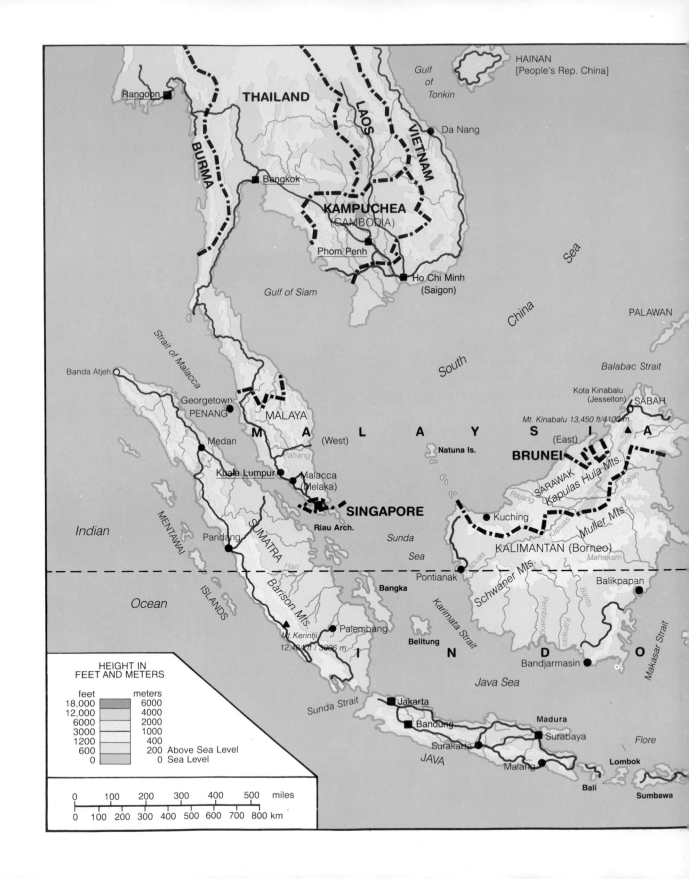

INDESIA — Political and Physical

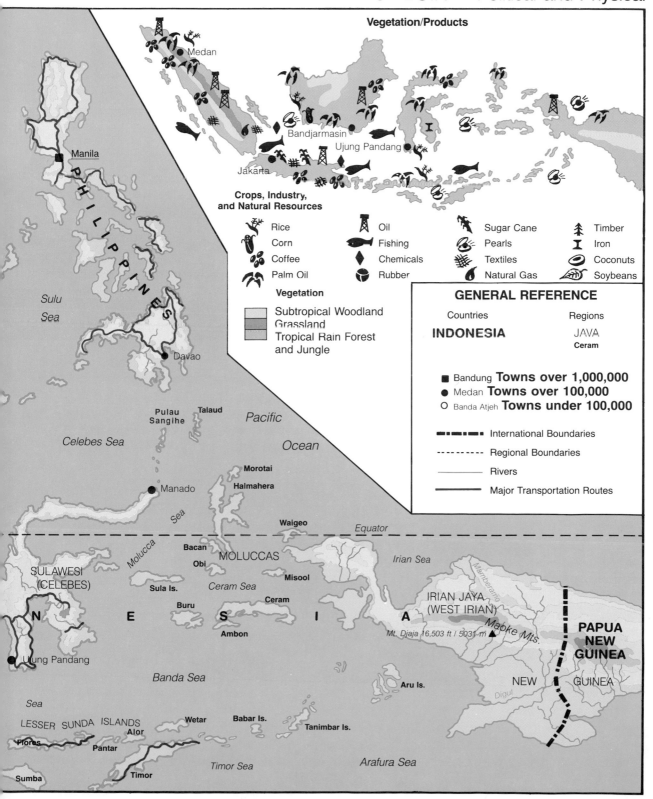

Vegetation/Products

Medan

Bandjarmasin

Ujung Pandang

Jakarta

**Crops, Industry,
and Natural Resources**

Rice		Oil		Sugar Cane	Timber
Corn		Fishing		Pearls	Iron
Coffee		Chemicals		Textiles	Coconuts
Palm Oil		Rubber		Natural Gas	Soybeans

Vegetation

Subtropical Woodland
Grassland
Tropical Rain Forest
and Jungle

GENERAL REFERENCE

Countries	Regions
INDONESIA	JAVA
	Ceram

■ Bandung **Towns over 1,000,000**
● Medan **Towns over 100,000**
○ Banda Atjeh **Towns under 100,000**

▬▬ International Boundaries

- - - - - Regional Boundaries

——— Rivers

——— Major Transportation Routes

*Sulu
Sea*

Manila

P H I L I P P I N E S

Davao

Pulau
Sangihe   Talaud

Pacific

Celebes Sea

Ocean

Morotai

Halmahera

Manado

Waigeo   *Equator*

Sea

Bacan

Obi   MOLUCCAS   *Irian Sea*

Molucca

SULAWESI
(CELEBES)   Sula Is.   *Ceram Sea*   Misool

Buru   Ceram

N   *Mamberamo*

E   S   I   A   IRIAN JAYA
(WEST IRIAN)

Ambon   *Mt. Djaja 16,503 ft / 5031 m* ▲   *Maoke Mts.*

**PAPUA
NEW
GUINEA**

Ujung Pandang

Aru Is.   NEW   GUINEA

Banda Sea   *Digul*

Sea

LESSER SUNDA ISLANDS   Wetar   Babar Is.   Tanimbar Is.

Flores   Alor

Pantar

Sumba   Timor   *Timor Sea*   *Arafura Sea*

Education

The government's goal is free and required education for all children between the ages of 6 and 14. This goal has not been reached. Although about 90% of the country's children are enrolled in primary school, most do not attend full time. Only about 15% of the children go to school after the age of 12. About 62% of the population can read. Less than 40% can read the country's official language, Bahasa Indonesia. The rate is higher for children between 6 and 16. This rate reflects the success of the government's recent concentration on education. Each of Indonesia's 27 provinces has at least one university or technical school. Many of its most accomplished students are educated in the West.

Traditionally, musicians and other performing artists were educated in their villages. Most still are today. The palaces and courts trained and supported many of the musicians who performed there. Since independence, the government has opened several Performing Arts Academies to help lower the cost of the performing troupes. Here students learn music, drama, and dance in a formal setting.

Sports and Recreation

Indonesians enjoy a wide variety of sports. Soccer is especially popular among young people, and bicycling is popular both for transportation and exercise. Indonesians also enjoy ping-pong, and they are known to be among the best volleyball and badminton players in the world. In the cities, people also enjoy going to movies, playing billiards, and shopping — all very social things to do. In rural areas, people haven't got as much entertainment lined up for them as in the cities. People do enjoy mobile movie shows that travel from town to town, setting up portable theaters in the fields.

Jakarta

With over 5 million people, Indonesia's capital is the country's largest city. It is also a city of contrasts. The older commercial part of the city is congested by day, deserted by night. North of this area is the old colonial city and its harbor, Sunda Kelapa. Here, near the end of the 16th century, Dutch and Portuguese traders competed for a foothold on Java, the island to which Jakarta is a gateway. Two architectural symbols of Indonesia's colonial days are the English Church, built during Britain's brief presence in Java (1811-16), and the "Portuguese" Church, begun by the Portuguese but completed by Dutch colonists in 1695.

To the east of the old colonial city are two *new* tourist spots — Ancol Dreamland, a sprawling entertainment center, and Tanjung Priok, Jakarta's new port. Another amusement area, "Mini-Indonesia," depicts the many national groups and cultures of Indonesia. Jakarta's six-lane "main street" — Jalan Thamrin — connects the old central square with Kebayoran Baru, one of the city's new suburbs. Many theaters, international hotels, office buildings, restaurants, and nightclubs lie along Jalan Thamrin, while just to the east are tree-lined streets with their old mansions from the colonial days.

Jalan Hayam Wuruk and Jalan Gajah Mada, two streets in the older section of Jakarta. The Ciliwung River divides many streets on its way to the Java Sea.

The traffic that clogs Jakarta's central city also contains signs of the old and new. New cars from Japan and West Germany compete for space with motorbikes and trucks, as well as vehicles built from parts and scraps of junked cars. Paying customers ride in taxis, motorized rickshaws, and double-decker buses. The buses are usually packed full, and they don't always come to a complete stop when they pick up and drop off passengers. The government plans for Jakarta to be free one day of the noisy motorized rickshaws. Around the fringes of the central area, bicycles and bike-pedalled rickshaws transport travellers at a busy if less noisy pace.

Taman Square, a huge parade ground with several boulevards crossing it, is a reminder of Indonesia's stormy political history. Towering above the square is the 400-foot (120-m) high Freedom Monument, which symbolizes the rebellion against the Dutch led by Indonesia's first president, Sukarno. Several blocks away from Taman Square is Banteng Square. Here stands a statue of a West Irian man breaking his chains — another symbol of the departure of the Dutch from Irian Jaya, formerly Western New Guinea.

Indonesians in North America

Nearly all Indonesians in Canada and the US are here as college students. Most students from Indonesia, especially graduate students, are supported by their government. Many live in university towns and larger cities. Because of its many colleges and universities, Boston has a large number of Indonesians. New York, Washington, Toronto, and Montreal also have sizeable Indonesian communities, and on the West Coast Los Angeles, San Francisco, and Vancouver have attracted many Indonesians, partly because of their milder climate. Los Angeles boasts North America's largest Indonesian community, with about 3,000 Indonesian residents.

More Books About Indonesia

Here are more books about Indonesia. If you are interested in them, check your library. They may be helpful in doing research for the "Things to Do" projects that follow.

Indonesia (A First Book). Poole (Franklin Watts)
The Land and People of Indonesia. Smith (Lippincott)

Glossary of Useful Indonesian Terms

adat (ah-DAHT) . . . . "custom"; the traditions and culture of a people
Apa kabar (AH-pah kah-BAR) . Hello
bahasa (bah-HAH-sah) . . . . "language"; Bahasa Indonesia is Indonesia's national language
bapak (BAH-pack) . . . . also *pak*; "father"; a respectful reference to any elder man; also for important younger men
batik (bah-TEEK) . . . . a kind of printing using cloth, dyes and wax
becak (BET-chalk) . . . . a pedicab, or rickshaw
belum (beh-LUM) . . . . "not yet"; used to avoid saying "no"
Bhinneka Tunggal Ika
(bih-NEE-kah tune-GAHL EE-kah) "Unity in Diversity," the Indonesian motto
bung (buhng) . . . . "brother"; a term of friendly respect for equals or people you don't know very well; used mainly in West Java. In Central and East Java, *mas* for men, *mbak* for women
gamelan (GAM-eh-lan) . . . . an orchestra
ibu (EE-boo) . . . . "mother"; a respectful reference to a woman
keroncong (keh-rawn-CHONG) ballads of Portuguese origin
merdeka (mare-DAY-ka) . . . . . . freedom
nona (NO-nah) . . . . polite reference to an unmarried woman
nyonya (nee-OH-nyah) . . . . polite reference to a married woman
orang (oh-RANG) . . . . human
wayang (why-YANG) . . . . a drama or play using dance and music

Things to Do — Research Projects

Indonesia gets over half its national income from government-owned oil production. Events in the world oil market can change quickly and affect the economic, political, and social well-being of Indonesia. As you read about Indonesia, or any country, keep in mind the importance of having current information. Some of the research projects that follow need accurate, up-to-date information. That is why current newspapers and magazines are useful sources of information. Two publications your library may have will tell you about recent magazine and newspaper articles on many topics:

The Reader's Guide to Periodical Literature
Children's Magazine Guide

For accurate answers to questions about such topics of current interest as Indonesia's development and the importance of oil to its development, look up *Indonesia* in these publications. They will lead you to the most up-to-date information you can find.

1. Many different ethnic and linguistic groups make Indonesia their home. Some of these groups also make up the population of other Asian countries. Pick one of the groups from Indonesia and see what other countries its people live in. How is their culture different in another country?

2. Often the success of a country's economic policies determines the success of its other programs. The economy supplies the money for the programs. How is the economy of Indonesia doing? How does this affect its educational programs?

3. Write a short report about a resource or industry important to Indonesia's economy. Be sure your information is current, at least within the last year.

4. Look up Indonesia in the *Reader's Guide to Periodical Literature* or the *Children's Magazine Guide*. Find articles that have been written recently, and report to your classmates about what has been happening in the last few months.

More Things to Do — Activities

These projects are designed to encourage you to think more about Indonesia. They offer interesting group or individual projects you can do at home or at school.

1. Batik has become a popular craft in Western countries. Check your library for craft books that tell how to do batik. Try to duplicate some of the designs on paper with paint or crayons. Make up some designs of your own.

2. How does your life compare to Doni's? Write an imaginary letter to him. Explain how you are the same or different.

3. How far is Jakarta, Indonesia, from where you live? Using maps, travel guides, travel agents, or any other resources you know of, find out how you could get there and how long it would take.

4. Check a library or bookstore for books about railroads in Indonesia. Compare their machinery and tracks to railroads in your country. You may want to take a trip to a railroad yard in your town. Compare pictures of the trains in this book with what you find there.

5. If you would like a pen pal in Indonesia, write to these people:

International Pen Friends
P.O. Box 65
Brooklyn, New York 11229

Be sure to tell them what country you want your pen pal to be from. Also include your full name, address, and age.

Index

63

Noah's Ark
AND OTHER BIBLE STORIES

BY REBECCA GLASER
ILLUSTRATED BY BILL FERENC AND EMMA TRITHART

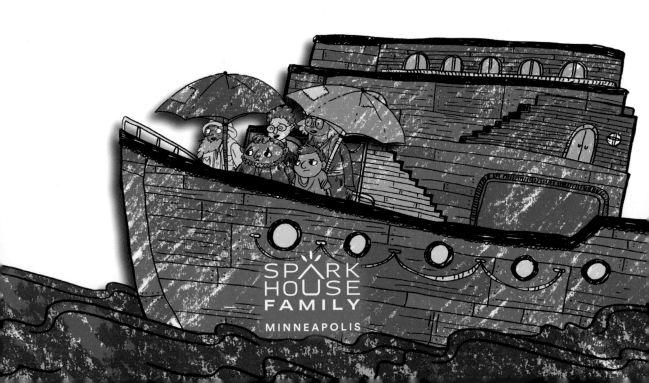

SPARK
HOUSE
FAMILY
MINNEAPOLIS

Contents

24 23 22 21 20 19 18 17 16 15   1 2 3 4 5 6 7 8
ISBN: 978-1-4514-9994-0

Book design by Toolbox Studios, Dave Wheeler, Alisha Lofgren, and Janelle Markgren
Illustrations by Bill Ferenc and Emma Trithart

Library of Congress Cataloging-in-Publication Data

Glaser, Rebecca Stromstad, author.
  Noah's ark and other Bible stories / by Rebecca Glaser ; illustrated by Bill Ferenc and Emma Trithart.
      pages cm. — (Holy moly Bible storybooks)
  Summary: "An illustrated retelling of the story of Noah's Ark and other common Bible stories"—Provided by publisher.
  Audience: Ages 5–8.
  Audience: K to grade 3.
  ISBN 978-1-4514-9994-0 (alk. paper)
1. Noah's ark—Juvenile literature. 2. Bible stories, English—Old Testament. I. Ferenc, Bill, illustrator. II. Trithart, Emma, illustrator. III. Title.
  BS658.G53 2015
  222.109209505—dc23
                         2015011203

Printed on acid-free paper

Printed in U.S.A.

V63474; 9781451499940; AUG2015

Creation

In the beginning, there was nothing, until God created the heavens and the earth. "Let there be light!" God commanded. And light sparkled across the water. God named light day and darkness night.

At the end of Day 1, God admired creation and said, "It is good."

On Day 2, God placed a bright blue sky high above the water.

Color in the sky.

Splish, splash! Dry land popped up from the water on Day 3. Green plants, tall trees, and colorful flowers burst from the earth.

4

God made the big, bright sun to shine during the day and the round, pale moon to shine at night. Stars twinkled all across the night sky on Day 4.

On Day 5, the water in the seas bubbled and gurgled and filled with fish. High in the sky, birds chirped and squawked and soared through the air.

Creeping and crawling, hopping and running, animals of every kind filled the earth on Day 6. Lions roared. Cats meowed. Horses neighed.

"Now," said God. "I will make people in my image." God created a man and a woman. God blessed them and put them in charge of caring for all of creation.

After six days of hustle and toil,
God took one day to rest.
God blessed Day 7 and made it holy.

With a smile and a laugh,
God looked over all of creation
and said, "It is very good!"

Adam and Eve

The first people God created were named Adam and Eve. They lived in the garden of Eden, where they had everything they needed. God had just one rule:

"You may eat fruit from any tree, except this one in the middle of the garden."

One grim day a serpent slithered up to Eve.

"Thisss tree has the sssweetest fruitsss!" the serpent hissed. *"Try sssome."*

"But God says no!" Eve replied. "If we eat that fruit, we will die!"

"You won't die," the serpent said. *"Eat the fruit from this tree in the middle of the garden. Then you'll know what'sss good and what'sss evil. You'll be like God!"*

Count the fruit on the tree.

Eve picked a fruit from the tree. **CRUNCH!** She took a juicy bite, then passed the fruit to Adam. **CHOMP!** Adam chewed and swallowed.

Gasp! Adam and Eve realized they were naked! They covered their bodies with leaves and hid.

"Where are you?" God called. Adam jumped up and blamed Eve. Eve leapt out and blamed the serpent. They hung their heads in shame.

God punished the serpent and Adam and Eve for breaking the one rule. After creating clothes for Adam and Eve, God sent them out of the perfect garden into the world. God would be with them there too.

Noah

God's creation grew and grew. But the people forgot about God. They fought with each other and destroyed things. They worshipped beings other than God.

"Do everything I have told you, and I will save you and your family."

Noah obeyed God. He sawed wood and hammered nails. Board by board, Noah built the ark.

15

Two at a time, animals waddled, stomped, and crawled onto the ark. When all the animals were aboard the ark, Noah and his family went inside.

Kerplunk, drip, splash! The rain began to fall.

Draw other animals that might have been on the ark.

It rained, and poured, and rained some more. The water rose higher and higher. The ark rocked back and forth. Everyone inside stayed dry.

After forty days, the rain stopped. Noah sent a dove to search for dry land.

17

When all the earth was dry,
God placed a rainbow in the sky.

"I will never flood the whole earth again,"
God promised. "This rainbow is a reminder
of my promise!"

Abraham

Abraham and his wife, Sarah, were faithful to God, but they were worried. Even though God had promised them a baby, they didn't have one. They were old—old enough to be grandparents or even great-grandparents. When would God's promise come true?

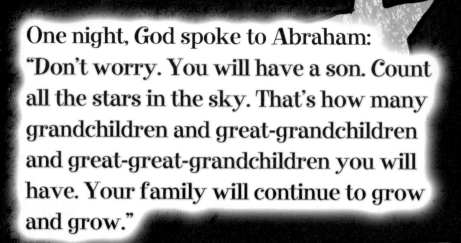

One night, God spoke to Abraham: "Don't worry. You will have a son. Count all the stars in the sky. That's how many grandchildren and great-grandchildren and great-great-grandchildren you will have. Your family will continue to grow and grow."

How many
stars do you
count?

21

Abraham and Sarah would have to wait many more years for their baby, but they trusted in God's promise.

Sarah and Abraham

One blazing hot afternoon, God sent three men to visit Abraham. When Abraham spotted them, he jumped up. "Hurry!" he called to Sarah. "Make bread for our guests!" Abraham rushed to prepare some meat.

Fill the sky with pictures of food you like to share with guests.

Abraham served the visitors, then sat down with them. **Splash!** The visitors washed their feet. **Slurp!** They drank the milk. **Chomp!** They ate the fresh meat.
"Where is your wife, Sarah?" the men asked.
"Soon she will have a son!"

24

But God keeps promises. Soon Sarah was expecting a child. When the baby was born, Abraham and Sarah named him Isaac.

Rebekah and Isaac

When Abraham and Sarah's son, Isaac, grew up, Abraham knew it was time for Isaac to get married.

Abraham went to his chief servant. "Go to my homeland," Abraham said. "Find a wife for my son Isaac."

The servant took the camels and traveled a long way to find Abraham's people.

28

After a long journey to Abraham's homeland, the servant stopped by a well and prayed. "God, help me find a wife for Isaac. If a woman offers a drink of water to me AND to my camels, let her be the one."

Just then, a woman named Rebekah came to the well. She offered water to Abraham's servant AND to his camels! The servant knew Rebekah would become Isaac's wife.

The servant asked Rebekah and her family if she would marry Isaac. They said YES! Rebekah traveled back with Abraham's servant.

Soon Isaac and Rebekah got married, and God blessed them.

More Activities

LOOK AND FIND

Find the numbers in the Creation story on pages 3–8.

God created for 6 days and rested on Day 7.

Find the  in the Adam and Eve story on pages 9–12.

God's punishment for the serpent was to make him move on his belly instead of legs.

Find the in the Noah story on pages 13–18.

A dove is often used to stand for peace.

Find the  in the Abraham and Sarah story on pages 23–26.

Sarah laughed when she heard she would have a baby. The name Isaac means "laughter."

Find the  in the Rebekah and Isaac story on pages 27–30.

Wells were popular meeting places for people in Bible times.

ACTION PRAYER

Creator God,

Thanks to you for what is dear. *(touch fingers to chin and lower hands to say "Thank you" in sign language)*

We'll take turns, shout out our cheer *(cup hands by mouth like a megaphone)*

For things we love, on Earth right here. *(point down toward the ground)*

I love _____ . *(act out or make the sound of each person's idea)*

Jump for joy. Shout hooray! *(jump up high)*

Bless us each and every day! *(hold up one finger on each syllable for seven total)*

Amen!

MATCHING GAME

Match the person from the Bible with the fact about them.

1. I was 600 years old when the flood began.

2. My name means "princess."

3. My name means "laughter."

4. I am the first woman God created.

5. I offered water to visitors, including camels!

6. I am the first man God created.

7. My name means "father of many nations."

1. Noah; 2. Sarah; 3. Isaac; 4. Eve; 5. Rebekah; 6. Adam; 7. Abraham